SHARK ATTACKS & SPIDER SNACKS

Roy Condy

Scholastic Canada Ltd.

Scholastic Canada Ltd.
123 Newkirk Road, Richmond Hill, Ontario, Canada L4C 3G5

Scholastic Inc.
555 Broadway, New York, NY 10012, USA

Ashton Scholastic Limited
Private Bag 94407, Greenmount, Auckland, New Zealand

Scholastic Australia Pty Limited
PO Box 579, Gosford NSW 2250, Australia

Scholastic Ltd.
Villiers House, Clarendon Avenue, Leamington Spa
Warwickshire CV32 5PR, UK

Canadian Cataloguing in Publication Data

Condy, Roy
  Shark attacks & spider snacks

ISBN 0-590-24622-4

1. Animals – Miscellanea – Juvenile literature.
2. Animals – Caricatures and cartoons – Juvenile
literature. I. Title. II. Title: Shark attacks
and spider snacks.

QL49.C65 1996   j591   C95-931821-6

5 4 3 2 1   Printed in Canada   6 7 8/9

To my wife, Margaret.

Burping Bossies

Ever win a burping contest? Ready for a real challenge? *Cows* might just be the world's champion belchers! That's because they're herbivores, which means they eat plants.

Vegetation is hard to digest, so cows rely on the bacteria living in their many stomachs to help break down the plant fibres. This action produces methane gas — a lot of methane gas. In fact, an average cow burps about 400 litres of gas a day. Multiply that by all the cows in the world and you have enough burps to produce more than 200 billion litres of methane gas a day!

Major Mom

Imagine a mom who's big and ugly, covered in scales, and has sharp, pointed teeth. That's what your mother would look like if you were a baby crocodile. And you'd be quite happy about it, because crocodiles are good mothers.

Adult Nile crocodiles are powerful predators, feared by most other creatures. But as babies they're an easy meal for lizards and herons as well as other birds of prey. If danger threatens, Mom seizes her young with her teeth and appears to swallow them — but they're perfectly safe. The kids are actually riding in her gular pouch, which is formed by the elastic skin that stretches across her lower jaw.

Once she has reached the shelter of the nearest pool, the mother crocodile opens her mouth, and out swim 20 or so little crocs, safe and sound.

Thanks, Mom!

Funky Fowl

Cranes really know how to get down. They have to: if the big birds didn't dance there wouldn't be any little cranes.

The ritual dance helps get the males and females "in the mood," so they are ready to mate at the same time. That way, the female will only lay fertile eggs, from which new cranes will hatch.

All crane couples — newly bonded young adults and older pairs that have been together for years — dance with the same enthusiasm. The cranes circle one another, bowing and tossing sticks and dirt. They run up and down, madly flapping their wings, and make amazing leaps straight up into the air — sometimes reaching a height of 3.5 metres!

Bug Bouncers

Ants can be violent when it comes to defending their homes. They'll assault enemies with bites, stings, sprays of burning acid or sticky glue.

But one type of Australian ant has a less deadly way of dealing with intruders. Like a bouncer at a rock concert, this ant physically tosses troublemakers out.

Unlike other ants, whose jaws are sharp, the Australian soldier has *blunt* mandibles. When its powerful jaws snap shut on an enemy ant's head, the effect is like squeezing a watermelon seed between your fingers. The victim is "squirted" up to 10 centimetres away — quite a distance for an ant.

The trespasser must get mighty mixed up — all of a sudden it finds itself somewhere else!

Baby Bullies

Got a brother or sister who picks on you? Be thankful you're not a golden eagle.

Golden eagle eggs hatch a few days apart. The first-born eaglet — being bigger and stronger — starts bullying its younger nest-mate as soon as it hatches. It pecks at its sibling, sits on it and chases it around. Sometimes the smaller bird is pushed right out of the nest and plunges to its death.

Even if the younger eaglet avoids such a fate, it usually dies of starvation anyway, because the older one gets all the food. To add insult to injury, the surviving eaglet often eats its dead sister or brother.

11

Tiny Terror

Ever hear of a small fry? Fry is a word meaning a young or small fish. Well, researchers at the Royal Ontario Museum have recently discovered the smallest fry in the world! The smallest member of the species *Trimmatom nanus* on record is only 8 millimetres long — the width of a pencil.

A member of the goby family, the pint-sized predator lives and hunts among the coral reefs of remote islands 1,500 kilometres south of India.

Trimmatom nanus must be a fearsome sight to its microscopic prey: if the little fish were the size of a 60-centimetre barracuda, its fangs would be almost 8 centimetres long.

Don't even think about making a meal of the world's smallest fish. You'd need over 3,600 of them to make up a quarter-pound fish burger!

Feline Fast Food

What's for dinner? If you were a tiger, it could be just about anything!

The biggest members of the cat family, tigers dine mostly on other large animals — like wild cattle, deer and pigs. But they aren't finicky.

If the main course isn't available, a tiger will make do with snacks. Monkeys, porcupines, birds, fish and turtles all make for satisfying munching.

And no prey is too small for the mighty hunter. Even tiny treats like termites and grasshoppers are mouth-watering to the voracious cats.

Marilea McAllister

Dung Delight

If dung beetles didn't really dig dung, our earth would be a smelly mess!

There are tens of millions of plant-eating animals in the world, which together produce an enormous amount of waste. A herd of 10 elephants, for example, can leave more than

900 kilograms of the stinky stuff every day. But a clean-up crew of busy dung beetles can have it all cleared away in a matter of hours. One dung beetle can move and bury more than 240 times its own size in a single night. And to make the job easier, certain species even form the manure into balls and roll it on home. A single beetle may only be 2.5 centimetres long, but it can transport a ball of dung the size of your morning grapefruit!

The beetles lay their eggs on the buried dung, which makes a nutritious meal for hatchlings.

SHOW-OFF!

Brain Bonkers

If you strapped on a beak and tried hammering on a tree trunk, you'd knock yourself silly. So why don't woodpeckers get brain damage when they drill for insects? Because they have built-in "crash helmets": their specially designed skulls.

Our brains float in a layer of fluid that absorbs everyday bumps and jolts. A hard blow, however, can cause the brain to smack against the inside of the skull, causing severe bruising. This is what happens when a boxer, for example, is knocked out.

But the woodpecker's skull is different. It contains very little fluid and fits the brain snugly, holding it firmly in place. The skull is made of thick, spongy bone, covered in a layer of resilient muscle. The result? A woodpecker can pound away at tree trunks as much as it wants, and its brain will stay safe and sound.

19

Coconutty Crab

If you ever visit a tropical isle, don't sit under a coconut tree — you might get conked by a crab.

The coconut crab is a land-dweller found on the islands of the southern Pacific Ocean. This resourceful creature comes equipped with powerful pincers, which it uses to crack open the shells of fallen coconuts to get at the meat inside.

Even if its favourite food is scarce on the ground, the clever crab doesn't go hungry: it can climb trees! It will scurry up a palm tree, snip off a coconut, then head back down to its reward lying on the sand below.

Unfortunately, coconut crabs are a tasty treat themselves, and on some islands they're all gone — people have eaten them all.

Fastest Web in the West

Imagine having to catch your supper with a lasso while hanging upside down on a trapeze. That's what a bolas spider does!

The clever creature first attaches a loose strand of cobweb beneath a branch to form a trapeze. Then it suspends a second strand of web, with a sticky blob on one end, from the middle of the trapeze. This second line is its trap line or lasso.

The spider hangs from the web by its hind legs, using its front legs to control the sticky trap line.

Once set up, it perches quietly on its tiny swing until a flying insect comes within close range. Then, suddenly, it propels itself toward the intended victim, swinging the sticky snare. Some spiders actually twirl the trap line like a cowboy's lasso, hoping to snag a passing morsel.

In either case, captured prey is quickly hauled in and hogtied!

Too Much Tooth

If you've ever had a hamster, gerbil or guinea pig, you know that they love to chew. In fact, all rodents — including squirrels, mice, rats, beavers and porcupines — are notorious gnawers. But why?

Unlike us, rodents have teeth that never stop growing! If they weren't worn down by all that chewing, they'd just get longer and

longer. Eventually they'd be so long the animal wouldn't be able to eat!

Rodent teeth are also self-sharpening: the front of the tooth wears down more slowly than the rest of it. With choppers that never get dull, a beaver can cut through a 40-centimetre-thick tree trunk in the course of one night!

I WARNED YOU ABOUT TAKING LONG NAPS!

25

Froggy Free-For-All

A poison-arrow frog has such poisonous skin that predators can't touch it — or they'd die. But the frogs can be pretty threatening to each other, too!

A male strawberry poison-arrow frog invading another's territory had better be prepared for a fight. Although they're less than 5 centimetres long, these brightly coloured inhabitants of the Amazon rain forest defend their tiny domains with fierce determination.

Chirping defiantly, two combatants will face off. Then they'll rear up on their hind legs, grasp each other in a wrestler's hug and begin to do battle.

The struggle may last up to half an hour, with each grappling frog attempting to wrestle the other into submission. Neither frog is harmed in the furious-looking fight; one of them simply gives up and creeps dejectedly away.

27

Bold Butterflies

If you've ever had a pretty butterfly fluttering around your head, you might have thought it was being friendly. In fact, it was probably an angry male, telling you to get lost!

Male butterflies are very aggressive when it comes to defending their territory. Females of the right species can enter the domain, but any males are immediately challenged and chased off the "property."

The silver spotted skipper is an especially scrappy species. It will attempt to shoo away any trespassers — even people!

Hidden Hulks

You've probably heard of the stealth fighter plane and the stealth bomber, right? Well, how about the stealth elephant? The word "stealth" means "secret action," which is exactly what the gentle giant uses to protect itself in the wild.

If you were hunting for elephants in the African bush, you'd probably expect them to be pretty easy to find. No way. A herd of the towering animals could sneak right up behind you — without making a sound!

Elephants have unique feet that are cushioned with thick pads of fat and fibrous tissue — they're a lot like big, round foam-rubber pillows. That's why elephants, with their average weight of over 4.6 tonnes, can move around so quietly.

Cannibal Kids

The praying mantis does more than just pray. It preys, too, on all kinds of other insects. It's also a cannibal, and won't hesitate to enrich its diet by eating its own kind.

Baby mantises — called nymphs — are especially prone to cannibalism. A newly hatched nymph is born hungry, and will quite happily make its first meal of a brother or sister. If food is scarce, the baby mantises will continue eating one another until only one is left!

Survival of the fullest, indeed.

33

Track-Star Turtles

Think all turtles are slow? Think again!

Soft-shelled turtles are the fastest turtles alive. They're pretty funny to look at: with their flat, round shells and pig-like snouts, they resemble pancakes with noses. But these are some serious turtles. Not only do they bite, but one North American species can outrun humans on level ground!

The clumsy-looking creature is just as quick under water. It can easily outswim a brook trout, the fastest of the freshwater fish.

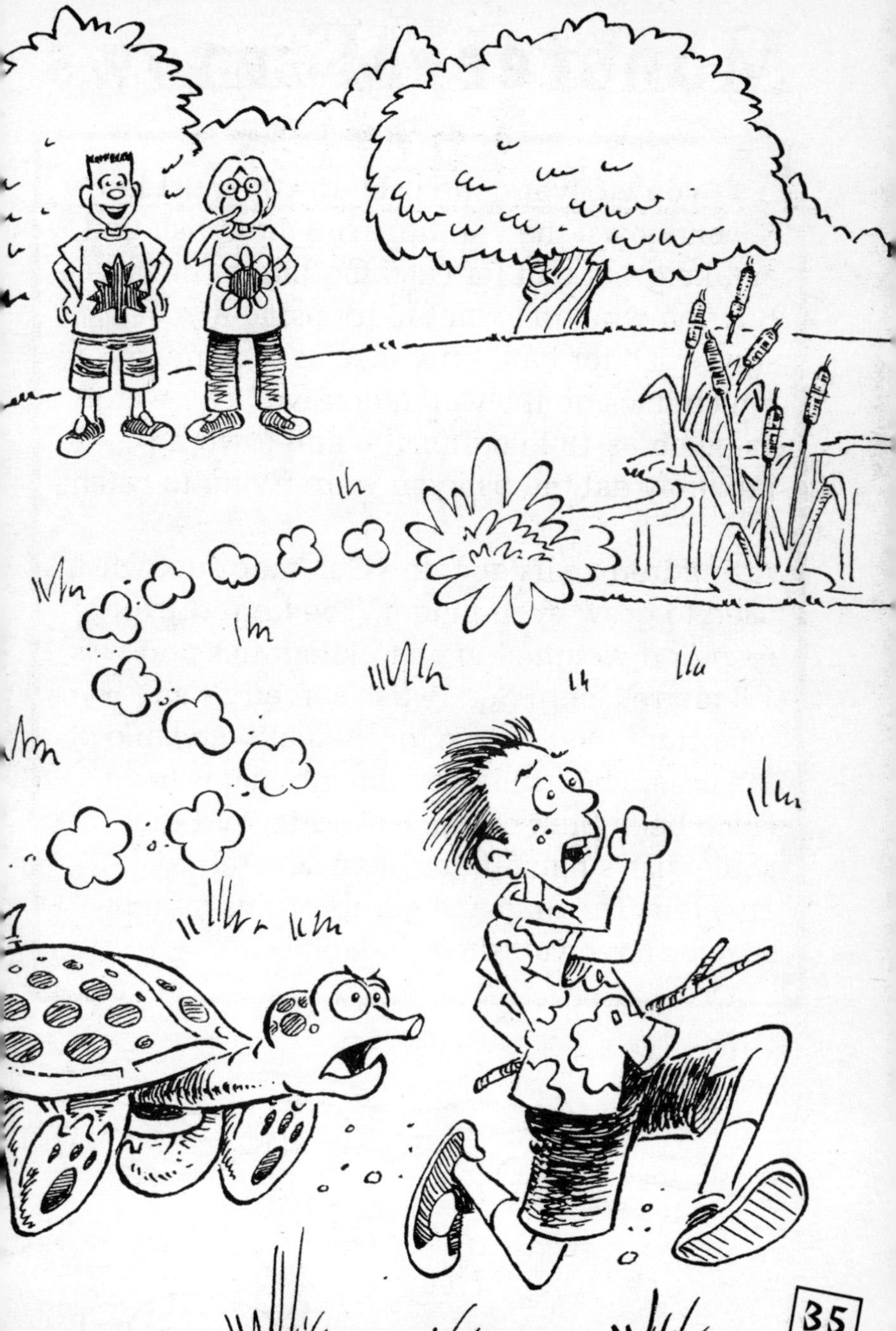

Monster Minnows

If you've ever gone fishing, you must know minnows: they're those tiny little fish that make great bait for catching bigger ones. But you wouldn't want to try using a squawfish for bait. This species of minnow, which lives on the Colorado River, can weigh as much as 18 kilograms — and it would probably eat the fish you were trying to catch!

A hundred years ago, the Colorado squawfish used to grow even bigger. The largest ever recorded weighed in at 45 kilograms and was 1.8 metres long! Squawfish served as an important food source for the native people of the area. Unfortunately, though, dams have since been built on the Colorado, and the squawfish's habitat has been severely affected. The amazing giants of this minnow species have vanished forever.

Vest-Pocket Vampire

We all know about vampires from movies — and we know that they're not real. Well, there are animal "vampires" that *are* real. But don't worry; they're only the size of mice!

The vampire bat is a flying mammal that lives in the southwestern United States and Central and South America. It flutters through the night sky, seeking out sleeping victims such as chickens, cattle, donkeys and deer.

A bite from its razor-sharp teeth is painless, and the vampire bat doesn't actually suck blood — it laps it up like a kitten at a saucer of milk.

Blood is the only food the bat can digest, and it will sometimes drink so much it can't fly. In fact, it can drink an amount equal to its own weight. But then, the average vampire bat only weighs 28 grams!

Dining
Dangerously

A swarm of sharks in the middle of a feeding frenzy is no pretty sight. They're vicious predators, and messy eaters, too. Bits of food floating in the water attract other sharks, and soon a whole pack of hungry sharks is fighting for a share of the kill.

In the confusion and poor visibility, one shark may accidentally bite another. Attracted by the scent of fresh blood, the others begin to bite at the new victim — and the injured shark is doomed.

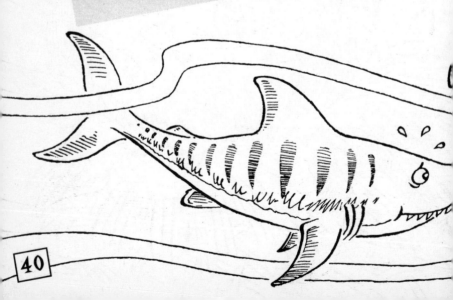

A feeding frenzy is so savage, a dying shark will continue to eat even as it is being eaten itself. The greedy creature will gobble down all it can — right up until the moment of death.

THAT'S THE LAST TIME I GO TO A FEEDING FRENZY WITH _YOU_ GUYS!

41

Phantom Fish

The hardest fish to see in the sea is the ice fish: it's practically transparent!

The odd-looking ice fish, which lives in the frigid waters of the Antarctic Ocean, appears to have no blood. That's because its blood is almost colourless. It doesn't have any red cells, which give blood its colour.

Red blood cells also carry oxygen through the body. But the strange blood of the ice fish contains very little oxygen — only one-tenth the amount other fishes have. So how does the ice fish exist without red blood cells and with so little oxygen? It's a mystery — scientists are baffled.

Squirmy Supper

Weevils are always sticking their noses where they're not wanted — namely, into our food.

The weevil, a member of the beetle family, uses its snout to drill into plants, fruits, nuts, rice and grains; it lays its eggs in the holes left behind. Every year weevils cause millions of dollars in damage.

In the days of sailing ships, weevils even went to sea. The basic food of seafarers back then was a thick biscuit called hardtack, which, after a while, would become infested with weevil grubs. Picky sailors would knock the grubs out of their hardtack before eating it, but they probably shouldn't have — eating the wiggling creatures would have been more nourishing.

Sometimes a weevil's nosy habits bring it to a sad end. If its feet slip while it's busily boring its way into the underside of an acorn or nut, the pest is left dangling helplessly by its "nose" until it dies.

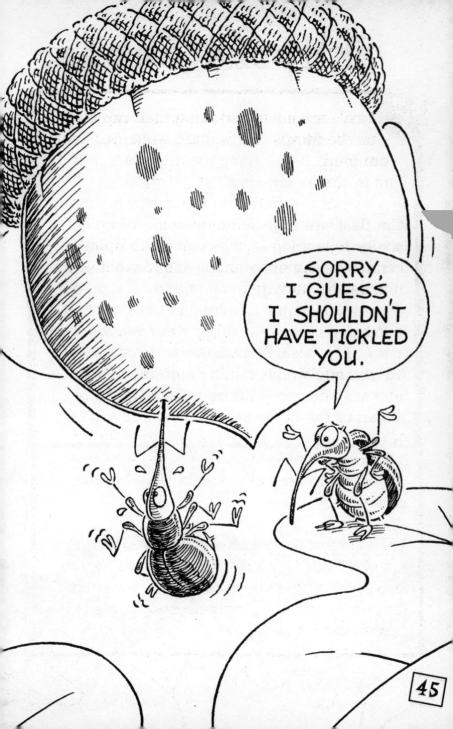

Flipping Fleas

Everyone knows that Superman can leap tall buildings in a single bound. But fleas are much better jumpers; they could put him to shame any day.

Cat fleas are especially awesome when it comes to leaping — they can cover up to 34 centimetres in one jump. That may not seem like much, but when you take their size into account, it's equal to a human hurdling half a kilometre.

To accomplish this mighty feat, the flea reaches an acceleration similar to that achieved by a moon rocket!

Blockhead Bugs

Some ant species have discovered a brainy way to keep intruders out of their homes — by using their heads.

Soldier ants in certain colonies have flat faces covered in thick armour. They use their heads like plugs to block the entrance to their nest. It's almost impossible for an attacker to force the living door open! If a blocking ant is pushed out of the way, a row of fellow soldiers is waiting right behind to quickly fill the gap.

Returning nest-mates identify themselves with a special signal. Only upon hearing it will the blocking ant back up to open the door.

A doorway too big for one guard to seal is no problem for the ants — they simply enlarge the door. Other soldiers then add their heads to the barricade until the gap is filled.

Obviously, two blockheads are better than one!

Toothless Attack Turtles

Like all turtles, the North American common snapping turtle is toothless. But don't let that fool you. The snapper, which grows to nearly a metre long, has a bad temper — and it's dangerous. It won't hesitate to attack anyone who gets too close, and strikes with the speed of a rattlesnake. The sharpened edges of its horny jaws can bite a finger off!

51

Piggyback Pals

When it comes to protecting itself, the hermit crab is unlucky: it doesn't have defensive armour like other crustaceans. No problem! It simply borrows the abandoned shell of a marine snail to use as shelter.

There *is* one enemy the crab isn't safe from, however. An octopus has no trouble yanking a crab out of its shell to make a tasty snack. So some hermit crabs adopt a poisonous sea anemone as a bodyguard. Stroking the anemone, the crab invites it to take up residence on the "roof," an offer the creature instinctively accepts. The anemone attaches itself to the top of the crab's borrowed shell, and off they go!

The relationship benefits both. The sea anemone, carried from place to place, has a greater chance of finding food, and the hermit crab is protected by the stinging tentacles of its bodyguard.

Mite Motel

Bet you didn't know that even bugs can be bugged by bugs. No joke! Insects like bees and beetles are often *infested* with mites.

Mites are tiny parasites related to spiders. Some species are so small they're invisible to the naked eye. A moth's ear, for example, can support an entire colony of mites with room for feeding, laying eggs and piling garbage.

The mites know well enough to take over only one ear, so their host won't go deaf. A moth that can't hear is easy prey for bats — and the mites have no desire to lose their comfy home.

Mega Meal

Imagine making a single scrambled egg — and feeding your whole family! Well, you could, if you had an ostrich egg. The world's biggest bird lays eggs that measure more than 20 centimetres long and weigh up to 1.5 kilograms. They're equal by volume to about two dozen hen's eggs!

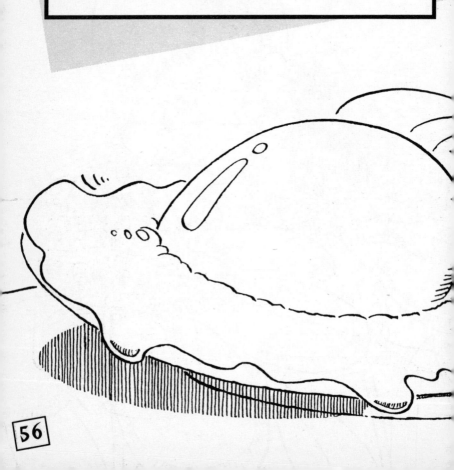

On the other hand, you and your family would starve on a bee hummingbird's egg. It's only 8 millimetres long — and would barely give a mouse a decent breakfast.

Prehistoric Pest

What do you do when you see a cockroach? Scream? Try to squash it? Maybe both. But people should treat the roach with more respect — it's a lot older than we are.

In fact, this amazing insect is one of the most primitive creatures on earth. Ancient fossils — 300 million years old — prove cockroaches were here long before the dinosaurs evolved. And they're still around, 65 million years *after* the last dinosaur disappeared.

They might outlast us too!

Micro Maids

Have you ever imagined monsters under your bed? Guess what? Monsters really *are* living there, and a lot more are *in* our beds.

The ugly critters have humped backs, eight legs, crab-like claws and bristles all over. They're called dust mites. But don't be afraid — they're so small you could easily squash a hundred of them between your fingers.

They eat dead skin, and humans shed billions of microscopic dead skin flakes every day. Up to 90 percent of house dust is our own skin!

Your bed is the best home in the world for dust mites. You provide them with food and keep them warm, and they're safe from the vacuum cleaner.

So when you slip between the nice clean sheets on your freshly made bed, think of the busy dust mites — up to two million of them — working hard to clear away the mess you're making.

At least you won't be lonely. Nighty night!

YOU EAT WHAT WE ALL EAT, MR. FINICKY. FINISH YOUR SUPPER!

61

Marilea McAllister

Roy Condy

Roy Condy discovered cartooning at the age of twelve, and has been drawing ever since. Besides TV shows and textbooks, Roy has illustrated many children's books, among them *How to Get Rid of Bad Dreams* and *Christopher, Please Clean Up Your Room*. And kids across Canada look forward to seeing his cartoons every year in the Scholastic *Student Organizer Diary*.

Roy lives in Toronto with his wife, Margaret, and their two cats, Camilla and Katie.